How to...
Lead the Prayers

A Training Course

Anna de Lange

Reader, Durham Diocese

Liz Simpson

Assistant Minister, South Molton, Devon

GROVE BOOKS LIMITED
RIDLEY HALL RD CAMBRIDGE CB3 9HU

Contents

Acknowledgments

We would like to thank members of GROW for their enthusiasm for this new style of booklet, and especially Chris Byworth, Mark Earey and Tim Stratford for their invaluable input.

The Cover Illustration is by Peter Ashton

First Impression April 2002
Reprinted with corrections March 2003
ISSN 0144-1728
ISBN 1 85174 494 0

Introduction

Why a booklet just on leading intercessions? Because leading people in prayer is a vital part of public worship but one for which there is little formal training available.

Those who preach go on courses, those who sing or play instruments practise and have rehearsals; too often those who pray are thrown in at the deep end with the service book and a prayer leaflet if they are lucky.

This is a book for using with a pen or highlighter in hand. As you read it we hope you will mark the things you agree and disagree with, highlight good ideas that you can use, and think about the issues that we raise. That is why there is scribble space at the end of each chapter.

You might like to go further and use the book and its questions in a group, or as part of a course for people who lead intercessions in your church. Use the scribble space as a memo for the contributions you feel you could make.

As we were writing this booklet we had in mind not clergy, not licensed ministers, not the 'professional,' but the men, women and children in our churches who week by week 'do the intercessions' in public worship. This is not to say the professionals may not pick up an idea or two! So we cover a wide range of is-

Too often those who pray are thrown in at the deep end with the service book and a prayer leaflet if they are lucky

sues, from 'why do it at all?' to 'how loud should I speak?' We hope that if you have got this far you will read what is helpful to you in your situation, file some of it in your mind for future use, and discard what is irrelevant or of no use.

Above all, our own prayer is that you will pick up things that help you to lead others into the presence of God in prayer, and that you will see prayers answered in the world and in your lives.

2

Why Pray?

This is such an obvious question that we often forget to ask it.

Why Pray At All?

◊ To bring our concerns to God.

◊ To follow Jesus' example.

◊ To draw the congregation together.

◊ To make a response to the rest of the service.

◊ To draw close to God ourselves.

◊ To provide a model for prayer.

In an all-age service this last point is particularly important.

A church service can be some people's only experience of prayer. Either we can show that prayer is difficult, only for the expert, and needs special words and attitudes, or we can show that good prayer is within their reach, whatever their age or experience.

Why Pray Together?

• **Corporate prayer is a powerful thing**. *'Again, truly I tell you, if two of you agree on earth about anything you ask, it will be done for you by my Father in heaven. For where two or three are gathered in my name, I am there among them.'*
Matthew 18.19–20

• It **helps us to respond** to what God is saying. If God has been speaking through the sermon, this should shape some of what we say back to God (corporately) in the prayers.

• It is a mark of a **healthy, growing church**. *They devoted themselves to the apostles' teaching and fellowship, to the breaking of bread and the prayers.* Acts 2.42

• When we pray together, **God is glorified**. *We always pray for you, asking that our God will make you worthy of his call and fulfil by his power every good resolve and work of faith, so that the name of our Lord Jesus may be glorified in you, and you in him.*
2 Thessalonians 1.11–12

What Are We Called to Pray For?

We pray together about things which concern the whole congregation, not simply for the leader's own agenda.

- **For our world**. God's people are called to bring the needs of their communities before him. *I urge that supplications, prayers, intercessions and thanksgivings be made for everyone, for kings and all who are in high positions.* 1 Timothy 2.1–2a

Praying in the context of a public church service is rather different from praying at home or in a small group. In a small group prayers can be more private and confidential, and personal concerns can safely be shared.

Remember—never use personal information about someone without asking them first, and do not be tempted to 'share' personal details.

- **For church leaders** and the mission of the church. The history of the church in the New Testament shows how important prayer is. *Pray for us as well, that God will open for us a door for the word, that we may declare the mystery of Christ.* Colossians 4.3 *Then after fasting and praying they laid their hands on them [Saul and Barnabas] and sent them off.* Acts 13.3

- **On behalf of all,** about the issues affecting the whole 'body' at a particular moment. *Pray in the Spirit on all occasions with all kinds of prayers and requests. With this in mind, be alert and always keep on praying for all the saints.* Ephesians 6.18

To Think About

❑ Why do *you* pray?

❑ Which of the reasons for praying together is most important in your church?

❑ Is there anything from the Bible passages you need to emphasize more in your church?

3 Is There a 'Best Way' to Pray?

The 'best way' to pray is one that leads people into the presence of God to do business with him.

So it is important to consider the style of the service and the shape of the prayers that will be used. What is best for a Prayer Book Holy Communion service is not likely to be best for the Pram Service!

The Style of the Service

The style and atmosphere of the worship should flow throughout the service, without bringing the congregation up short (unless such an effect is deliberate and part of the 'plot'!). If you are leading the prayers, you need to reflect on the style and type of service, and on the sort of people (age, culture and so on) who are likely to be there.

Nevertheless, the pattern of prayer is fairly constant, and *Common Worship* gives helpful guidance. The Service of Holy Communion (on p 174 of the main volume) reminds us not to be church-centred, but to remember the world and our community:

> *The prayers usually include these concerns and may follow this sequence:*
> * *The Church of Christ*
> * *Creation, human society, the Sovereign and those in authority*
> * *The local community*
> * *Those who suffer*
> * *The communion of saints*

The introduction to A Service of the Word (p 23) speaks more of the style and presentation but also points out the importance of including thanksgiving. This is because there is no eucharistic prayer to supply this element in the service.

> *There are many different options for this part of the service. These range from a series of Collect-type prayers to congregational involvement in prayer groups, visual and processional prayers, with responsive forms and a number of people sharing the intercessions in between. But, whatever the form, it is essential that the Prayers also include thanksgiving.*

The Shape of Our Prayers

There are two basic shapes of prayer:

- A series of short prayers or topics for prayer (sometimes called 'biddings') with responses in between and one 'Amen' at the very end. This is sometimes referred to as a 'litany' form. If you use a printed litany you can add your own topics, or extra prayers, or times of silence.

> In a *litany* a variety of patterns can be used:
> ◊ bidding—silence—set words—response
> ◊ bidding—leader's prayer—silence—set words—response
> ◊ leader's prayer—silence—set words—response
> ◊ series of biddings and silence—whole set prayer

- Several longer prayers, each with its own 'Amen.' These might be structured as 'collect' prayers but they do not have to be. You can still use biddings and silence before each prayer.

> A *Collect* is a prayer which gathers together, summarizes or 'collects' up the prayers of the congregation and is said by the minister with all responding *Amen* at the end. A Collect is usually written around a set pattern:
> ◊ address to God: 'Almighty God,' 'Loving Father,' 'Tender God.'
> ◊ reason for our confidence in asking, which might be something about God's character or actions or what God has done in the past: 'you are always more willing to give than we to ask' or 'you rescued your people and brought them into the Promised Land.'
> ◊ what we want God to do for us: 'keep us…'
> ◊ sometimes: 'so that…'
> ◊ ascription: 'in the name of…'

Examples of both types of prayer are given in *Common Worship* (p 281ff), but it is useful to know how they are constructed, so that you can write your own. The key to both shapes is that they have a predictable rhythm, which helps a congregation to engage with them. If you write your own prayers, make sure that the pattern of prayer is consistent (for example, bidding—prayer—response) throughout.

There is nothing sacrosanct about prayers printed in a book! They are there to be used, if they fit your situation, or to mine for good phrases and ideas, or as patterns for writing local prayers which express what the congregation want to say. Even when using *Common Worship* prayers in a formal service you do not have to include every word, and the order can be changed to fit in with the shape of prayer which you are using.

Using Responses

It is a good idea to use some response which people can join in, as this helps them to take part in the prayer and prevents it being just words spoken by the leader. Responses can be said or sung (or even done) and can be varied according to the season or theme of the service.

Why not sing the responses? You could use Taizé or Iona music, or a verse or refrain from one of the day's hymns.

Your church probably has familiar responses, but they can be varied, as long as the congregation are told clearly what the response is to be. You can introduce new responses by saying, for example, 'After the words Lord of light you respond Shine into our lives.' Then let them practise immediately by repeating the cue line for them to respond. Simple responses do not need printing on a service sheet, but do not expect people to remember a new one of more than five or six words.

Have you ever considered asking people to clap or wave instead of making a spoken response?

There are various responses suggested in *Common Worship* and more in *Patterns for Worship* but it can be good to tailor your own to the focus of the rest of the service. For example, in Pentecost you might want to pray something like 'Holy Spirit, come into our lives' or 'Spirit of God, renew your creation.' Remember to make the trigger words strong and distinctive, and take care not to use them where you *do not* want a response.

To Think About

❑ How many different types of service are there in your church?

❑ Are the prayers 'stuck' in one style or shape?

❑ How many different responses do you use?

4 Where Do I Start?

You have been asked to lead the prayers. You have a blank sheet of paper, and an equally blank mind. Where do you start?

By praying yourself, that God will show you what are the concerns close to his heart. Ask him to give you a structure, an idea, an activity—a hook to hang the prayers on this week.

Before you even put pen to paper, think about the things in this checklist.

❏ Have you read the readings? You can use them as a basis for some prayer: 'Father, thank you…' [for what a certain verse says] or 'Please help us…' [to do what the verse says].

❏ Have you looked at the themes of readings, the sermon title or the seasonal theme?

❏ Ask the preacher or service leader if there are specific things to pray for. Some of the praying should relate to the sermon, but beware of re-preaching it point by point!

> *Use paper shapes for whatever happens to fit the theme— church building, hands, leaves —and ask people to write items for prayer on them (or draw a picture, for the little ones). At the end of the prayers, invite them to bring them up and attach them to a display board (perhaps also in a relevant shape)—perhaps while singing a prayerful hymn or chorus.*

❏ What is happening in the world? Remember long-term trouble-spots as well as the week's headline news.

❏ Read the church notices (if any), or talk to the minister or another church leader for more information.

❏ Make sure you know if there are special events like baptisms, and whether there are likely to be lots of children or strangers present.

> *Or try the last idea with post-it notes, or with paper chain slips that can then be linked into a prayer chain.*

❏ Have you looked at the Anglican or diocesan prayer cycle giving suggestions for prayers? Or is it Sea Sunday or Education Sunday or is there some other focus of interest to your church?

❏ Remember what was prayed for last week. Is there anything for which you can give thanks?

❏ Decide on the topics for prayer. You do not need to pray for everything every week. The danger of having too many topics is that you will move from one to the next too quickly for the congregation to keep up.

❏ Think and pray about what the congregation can agree to say 'Amen' to. It is important to be clear and specific, especially when praying for difficult situations or for individuals who are ill. But do not push people into praying something they do not believe can happen.

It Is A Good Idea To:

✔ Use natural language so that the congregation can understand and mean their 'Amen.'

✔ Keep the prayers short. Three to five minutes is usually OK, ten is not (unless the service is one with a particular prayer focus). It can help if you sometimes take one section and elaborate on it, whilst keeping the others simpler.

✔ Nevertheless, repetition can be valuable (we thank you for…we thank you for…) as can good rhythm.

✔ Make sure that people know how and when to end each prayer. If 'Amen,' lead up to it with a recognized phrase.

Language

• Address prayer to God and biddings to the people.

• Be consistent and accurate in addressing Father, Son or Holy Spirit. For example, do not thank the Father for dying on the cross.

• Be economical with words. Use as few as you need, without padding. Try writing out what you intend to say, and then use a red pencil!

• Words to avoid: 'just' (as in 'Let's just pray…'), 'really,' 'overrule…' Use ordinary everyday language, not Christian jargon or Prayer Book language (unless using ancient prayers!).

✔ Distinguish between intercession, thanksgiving, confession and adoration. In the Communion Service, adoration, thanksgiving and confession usually come in other places, so this time is meant for intercession. In a Service of the Word, check what else is happening in the course of the service.

Some Definitions

Intercession: asking God to help others

Thanksgiving: thanking God for what he has done

Confession: saying sorry to God

Adoration: praising God for who he is

✔ Use silence for people to catch up on a rapid succession of ideas or visual images. Make it clear what you are doing and what the silence is for. Leave enough time, maybe 30 seconds—count, as it will feel longer than you expect.

Use pictures, projected on a screen or enlarged on a photocopier and held up. Suggest that the congregation keep their eyes open so they can see what or whom they are praying for.

✔ Find out where in the service the prayers come so you know whether you need to respond to what has gone before.

✔ Include a phrase such as 'and there are others *(silence)*' if you pray by name for individuals who are sick, in need or bereaved (such as those on the news-sheet). This enables people to bring others to God.

✔ Listen to the news and read the papers. Others will have done, and will expect you to include prayers for victims of a natural disaster, or to mention a national figure who has died.

But Avoid:

✗ Chatting to the congregation or repeating the news bulletins. Keep any introduction or bidding very short, and use the prayer itself (or the silence) for doing business with God.

✗ Using the prayers to preach at people or make value judgments. In prayer you are addressing God, not the congregation.

✗ Switching between a set of separate prayers and a set of biddings with responses that conclude with a prayer. Use one form or the other all through.

✗ Juggling a lot of books. It is better to write the prayers out on one piece of paper, then you do not get lost, and the microphone does not pick up lots of rustling as you sort papers.

✗ Assuming that everyone knows something by heart (even the Lord's Prayer or the Grace). If you include a prayer for everyone to join in, give a page or a reference, and lead into it really slowly.

To Think About

❏ Have you or your church got a checklist similar to the one here?

❏ Is there anything you could add to your preparation of the prayers?

❏ Think about your own use of rhythm, repetition and silence.

5

What Do I Pray About?

Be relevant to all the groups in your congregation.

Talk to people. What are they concerned about? What are their worries? What world issues bother them?

- Many children are surprisingly aware of worldwide issues. They feel the hurts and the tragedies, they see the trauma on television, but they feel helpless. They can pray.

- Remember your congregation. Are GCSE results due out this week? Does the mother and toddler group have an outing? Does a new term start? Are there elections? Pray for the events and for those involved and affected by the outcome.

- Remember the less obvious as well as the obvious. Pray for singles as well as families, for chronically ill as well as emergencies, for the healthy as well as the sick, for faithful helpers (church cleaning teams?) as well as special events, for the retired and unemployed as well as workers.

- But do not get parochial. Remember that the world goes on outside the church building and the church family.

- And do *not* be tempted to preach or make political points. You are helping people to talk to God, not haranguing them.

To Think About

❏ What are the interests and ages of your congregation?

❏ Do the prayers take account of the world outside the church as well as the church family?

Do Something Different!

6

How You Pray

- Try a time of open prayer, perhaps encouraged by specific biddings, such as 'Would two or three people pray for...' If you have a large building it may be difficult to hear people, and so an alternative is to invite people to join 3 or 4 others and pray in small groups.

- Would it be a good idea to have one long slot for the prayers, or two or more shorter ones?

Encourage people towards open prayer by enlisting some runners. Anyone with a concern that they want to pray for puts up their hand, and whispers it to a 'runner.' The runner relays the prayer to the people leading interces-sions, and they pray aloud, briefly and simply.

Action As You Pray

- Use something visual—a job application form, photographs of your link missionary, or pictures projected onto a screen. Bring newspaper cuttings, or have something for people to hold such as pebbles or candles.

Try using balloon prayers. Before the service write single-sentence prayers on slips of paper, insert each one in a balloon, then blow the balloon up and tie it. People bat the balloons about until the music stops—then the person holding each one pops it, and reads the prayer it contains aloud. Noisy but fun, and can get people who would not dream of praying aloud to take part in the prayers.

- Use music to create an atmosphere; perhaps as a background to spoken prayer or silence.

- Suggest using various positions: standing, kneeling, sitting, joining hands, keeping eyes open.

- DIY. Distribute paper and pens and ask people to write their own prayers, probably for something specific. They could be on shaped pieces of paper, such as leaves which are then fixed on a large tree shape, or they could be brought up to the Communion table at the end of the prayers.

What You Pray

- Use prayers written by others, maybe by members of the Youth Group or Mothers' Union as well as from books.

- Use a tape, for instance with a message from an absent member.

- Use congregational responses other than 'Amen,' or 'Hear our prayer,' either spoken or sung. Taizé and Iona resources are a good place to start.

Pray for the world. Get hold of a large map to spread on the floor (Early Learning Centre do one); as you pray for people in different parts, light a candle (or ask someone with connections in that place to do so) and place it on the relevant area on the map. Be careful the base is not hot and does not melt the plastic!

- Use song-prayers such as 'Beauty for Brokenness' (Graham Kendrick) or 'Make me a channel' (based on St Francis).

Invite everyone to write their name on a place card as they come into church. At the prayer time, give these out randomly so everyone has a card with someone else's name. Invite them to pray silently for this person (or in small groups if you like)—and suggest they take the card home with them and pray for the person during the week.

This can really capture children's imagination—in one household the person was prayed for every meal time for a week!

- Pray for different 'sectors' as a regular feature for one sector each week, or repeated several times for different people in one service. Choose one type of person (such as mothers, Sunday School children, those taking exams). Ask the whole congregation to stand *except* those being prayed for, and lead in a prayer (or a time of open prayer). People nearby can touch those sitting if appropriate.

- Take one particular situation or theme and pray about many different aspects. Pray about a recent natural disaster: for those injured, bereaved, homeless; for those working as rescuers; for worried relatives and friends; for those trying to organize relief; for aid agencies; for doctors, nurses, hospitals; for the local and national government; for other governments and their response.

- Pray for missions—for local outreach, for those living in unsympathetic homes, for your church's link missionaries, for national initiatives, for missionary organizations.

- What about using the Litany—originally used in a procession (*Common Worship*, pages 111, 284, 286).

- Use guided silence—but good directions are important, and visual aids help to concentrate the mind.

Use the architecture—have a mini-procession around the church to strategic points (such as the door, font, crèche, choir stalls, pulpit…) and pray for who or what you associate with them, such as baptism families and children, mission, new Christians and non-churchgoers, those who lead music or preach….

Or use the stained glass windows, if they depict suitable stories, to spark off prayers. Or use the wording of a banner as a response.

Where You Pray

- Consider standing somewhere other than at the front. If there is a radio microphone it is easy to stand at the back of church, or half-way down the nave, or even to lead the prayers from 'within' the congregation. In this way the prayers are seen to be offered up by the people.

With a small group (or several) bring a ball of string and ask them to throw it to each other, so that they end up all connected. Then they pray (aloud or silently) for the people at the other ends of the bit of string they are holding. This works well with teenagers.

- Move around the church (see box above) or walk around outside and pray for the areas of the community which you can see, such as farmers, businesses or schools.

Who Prays

- Use different voices—from different people, that is! Ask a group to lead the prayers, for example, a children's group or a family. Make sure that each person has prayers suitable for their age, understanding and interest.

When Words Simply Will Not Do

There are times when words are inadequate, but space, silence and symbols can be very important. Maturity sometimes recognizes that we have to start in silence before God, before progressing to sighs and groans (Romans 8.26).

Short biddings can be used, along the lines of 'Let us hold before God all who are involved in...'; 'Let us hold before God all rescue workers in...' leaving plenty of silence afterwards for people to pray their own thoughts.

It might help if you leave space to do something symbolic, such as lighting a candle or dropping a stone in a bowl of water. People may feel more comfortable if there is a background of very quiet music (organ, piano or recorded).

Have You Thought About? (to be looked at before Saturday evening!)

- If you want to include a song as a prayer, or music behind the words, remember that you will need to consult the musicians.

- If you want to use an OHP, it needs to be set up so people can see it, and the slides need to be clear and preferably brightly coloured.

- If you are using visual aids, have you everything you need? If you are asking people to write prayers, have you enough paper and pens and have you thought how to collect them up at the end?

Have a bowl of burning coals and another containing incense. Invite people to take a few grains of incense and add them to the burning coals as they pray for specific people or situations.

Or lay out white tiles (about a square metre is ample) to form a cross on the floor, and light a large candle in the centre or at the head. Have night-lights or similar candles nearby, and invite people to come and light one from the large candle and place them on the cross as they say a silent prayer.

Ideas like these cannot be hurried, and you need to leave time afterwards for people to sit and watch the smoke or the lights. Both work well with teenagers, and can be very effective with the right Bible passage at any time.

To Think About

❑ Is there one idea from these pages that you could use next time you lead the intercessions?

❑ How might you encourage other people who lead intercessions to be more creative in the way they do it?

7

Time and Motion

- Remember to find out the latest news before you come to church so that you can include any last-minute news that is important, especially a disaster or the death of a notable person. Remember, Princess Diana died in the early hours of a Sunday…

- Decide where you want to stand or kneel to lead the prayers. Remember, you must be heard by all the congregation, and should use the microphone if there is one, so that might restrict you.

- Sit at the end of a row where you can easily get to where you will be leading from.

- Make sure that you know where your 'bit' comes in the service. If there is a hymn immediately before, move into place during the last verse. At Holy Communion services the intercessions usually come after the creed or the confession; move promptly once that is finished. Otherwise, relax and go with the style of the service—a pause never did any harm.

Using a Microphone

If there is a microphone, use it even if you have a loud voice. There may be an induction loop to help the hard-of-hearing, and some churches record parts of the service. In both cases the microphone is the pick-up for the system.

Microphones differ, so take guidance on the one in your church. However, some general principles usually apply:

- stand so that you are speaking towards the microphone;

- normally there is no need to be closer than about two feet;

- ignore the fact that the microphone is there at all. It is there to reinforce your voice, not to do all the work for you.

If you speak as if you had no amplification, you will be doing fine.

- Allow the congregation to settle before you start speaking. This may take quite a while; watch to see when people are ready. If you ask people to sit, stand or kneel there are always two shuffles, one as they do what you have asked and another as they get comfortable. Before speaking wait until the second shuffle has died down.

- Take your time, speak slowly, and include plenty of pauses.

- Afterwards, do not rush back to your seat. Pause for a moment, and then return quietly and gently.

How Do I Make Sure I Can Be Heard?

Whatever part you are playing in the service, and however small you feel it to be, you play an important part in helping others to approach God. If no-one can hear what you say, then every word is utterly wasted. So it is important that you make your voice carry.

The larger the building the slower you need to speak. When a church is full of people the sound is absorbed very easily and tends not to be heard clearly, so you have to take extra care. Here are some hints to help you.

- Hold your notes and your head up, looking out rather than down.

- Imagine that you are talking to someone right at the other end of the church. That way you will 'throw' your voice. If you do not know what this feels like, go into the empty church with a friend and hold a conversation with one of you at each end of the nave.

- Stand straight, well-balanced, feet apart, no shuffling. If you have your weight on your toes rather than your heels you will find breathing easier.

To Think About

☐ Do you (or someone else) need to practise speaking in church? Ask someone to come with you and give you some constructive criticism.

☐ Would it be of value to your intercessions team to have a training session based on this booklet?

And Finally...

Pray thankfully...*1 Timothy 2.1*

Pray briefly...avoid long, drawn-out details.

Pray clearly...use words and ideas people will know.

Pray specifically...ask God to do definite things.

Pray expectantly...something's going to happen.

Pray humbly...you do not have all the answers. *2 Chronicles 7.14*

Pray boldly...that is our privilege. *1 John 5.14*

Avoid using prayers to teach people points you think they need to know.

A Thought to Take Away

If you end up feeling you could have done better,
you are a normal human being.

The church is the family of God,
not an audience,
and will be more tolerant
(and maybe unaware) of mistakes
than you will be.

God honours those
who have honoured him
in their preparation
and in their heart.

Further Resources

8

Sue Wallace	*Multi-sensory Prayer*
	Over 60 innovative ready-to-use ideas
	(Scripture Union, 2000, ISBN 1 85999 465 2)
John Pritchard	*The Intercessions Handbook*
	Creative ideas for public and private prayer
	(SPCK, 2000, ISBN 0 2810 49793)
Judith Merrell	*101 ideas for Creative Prayers*
	(Scripture Union, 1995, ISBN 0 86201 954 0)
Raymond Chapman	*Leading Intercessions*
	Prayers for Sundays, Holy Days and Festivals,
	Years A, B and C
	(Canterbury Press, 2000, ISBN 1 85311 377 8)

And there are resources based on the three years of the lectionary, such as:

Susan Sayers	*Living Stones: Prayers of Intercession*
	(Kevin Mayhew)
Susan Sayers	*Living Stones: Complete Resource Book*
	(Kevin Mayhew)
Diana Murrie and	*Worship Through the Christian Year*
Hamish Bruce	(National Society/CHP)

Common Worship resources already available and forthcoming including the main volume ('the black book'), *Patterns for Worship*, *Daily Prayer* and the seasonal material.

There are many collections of prayers, often in paperback and often very affordable. Browse in your local Christian bookshop to find what is available and suitable for your situation.